HEIGHTS

Y0-CAE-981

teddy bears 1 to 10

MEADE HEIGHTS
MEDIA CENTER

25890

susanna gretz

teddy bears 1 to 10

FOUR WINDS PRESS   NEW YORK

1 teddy bear

2 old teddy bears

3 dirty old teddy bears

4 teddy bears in the wash

5 teddy bears
on the clothesline

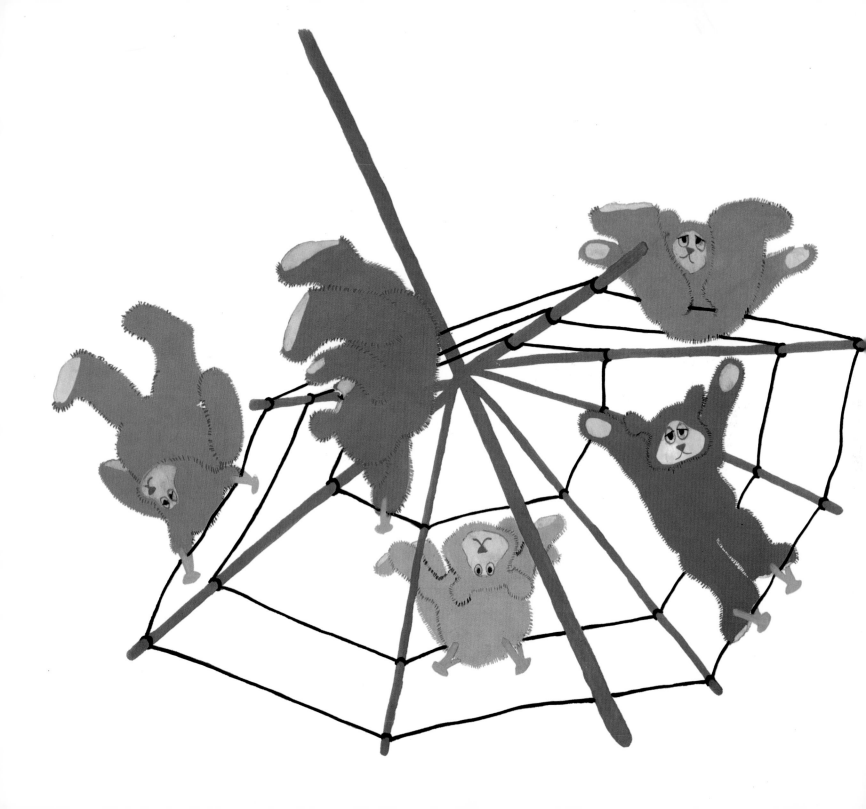

6 teddy bears
on the radiator

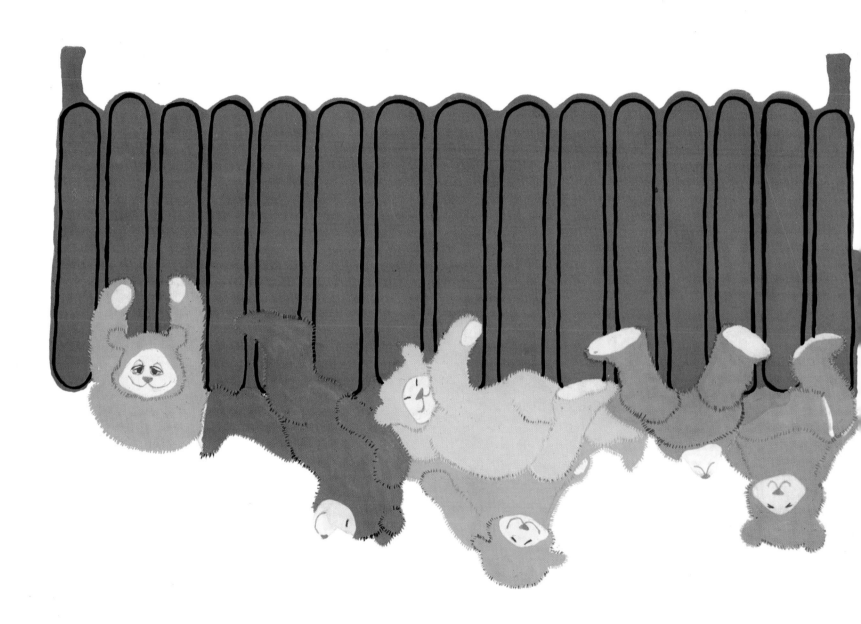

7 teddy bears
at the cleaner's

8 teddy bears
at the dyer's

9 teddy bears
on the bus

and 10 teddy bears
home for tea

Copyright © Ernest Benn Limited 1969

All rights reserved. No part of this book may be reproduced
or transmitted in any form or by any means, electronic
or mechanical, including photocopying, recording, or
by any information storage and retrieval system, without
permission in writing from the Publisher.

Four Winds Press
Macmillan Publishing Company
866 Third Avenue, New York, N Y 10022
Collier Macmillan Canada, Inc.

Printed in Great Britain

First published in 1969 by Ernest Benn Ltd, London

First Four Winds Press edition 1986

10 9 8 7 6 5 4 3

Library of Congress Cataloging-in-Publication Data

Gretz, Susanna. Teddy bears 1 to 10.

Summary: As teddy bears are washed, dried, take the
bus, and have tea they introduce the numbers one to ten.
1. Counting—Juvenile literature. [1. Counting]
I. Title. II. Title: Teddy bears one to ten.
QA113.G74 1986   513'.2 [E]   86-4795

ISBN 0-02-738140-4

Printed in Singapore by Imago Publishing Ltd

569232 01186 54866A 04956E   003

MEADE HEIGHTS ELEM SCHOOL
ANNE ARUNDEL CO PUBLIC SCHOOLS

9/96   # 11.86

GRE
513   Gretz, Susanna.
             Teddy bears 1 to 10

25890

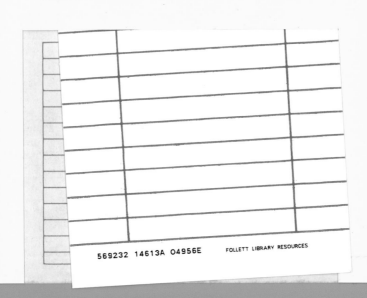

569232 14613A 04956E   FOLLETT LIBRARY RESOURCES